steaming
steaming

steaming

steaming

steaming
steaming
steaming
steaming
healthy food from China, Japan, and Southeast Asia

Elsa Petersen-Schepelern   *photography by William Lingwood*

RYLAND
PETERS
& SMALL
LONDON   NEW YORK

First published in the United States in 2002
by Ryland Peters & Small, Inc.
519 Broadway, 5th Floor
New York, NY 10012
www.rylandpeters.com

10 9 8 7 6 5 4 3 2 1

Library of Congress Cataloging-in-Publication Data

Petersen-Schepelern, Elsa.
  Steaming : healthy food from China, Japan & South East Asia /
  by Elsa Petersen-Schepelern.
    p. cm.
  ISBN 1-84172-293-6
    1. Cookery, Asian. 2. Steaming (Cookery) I. Title.

TX724.5.A1 P48 2002
641.7'3'095—dc21   2001048836

Printed and bound in China

Senior Designer Steve Painter
Editor Jennifer Herman
Production Meryl Silbert
Art Director Gabriella Le Grazie
Publishing Director Alison Starling

Food Stylist Julz Beresford
Stylist Liz Belton
Photographer's Assistant Emma Bentham-Wood

Notes

All spoon measurements are level.
Ingredients in this book are available from larger supermarkets,
speciality stores, and, especially, Asian stores and markets.

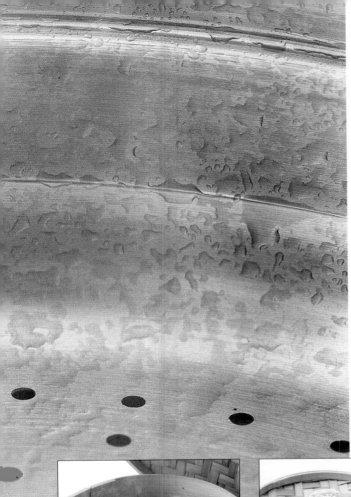

Contents

Steaming is the new stir-fry ...

Think of steaming as the new stir-fry. It keeps all the freshness, goodness and color of the food, in the same way as stir-fry—but you don't need any oil! In this low-fat-obsessed age, that can only be a good thing.

Steaming really is one of the healthiest ways of cooking, in which very few nutrients are lost. It's especially good for delicate foods, such as fish, seafood, and chicken—and comes into its own with vegetables.

Steamers are available in many forms. Some of the simplest and best-looking are the elegant bamboo steamers, as shown on this page, sold very cheaply in Asian markets and stylish cookware and interiors stores. These are available in many sizes—from huge ones, which can double as serving trays for parties, right down to the single-serving minis you see in dim sum restaurants. I also have a multi-layered Vietnamese metal steamer (pages 2 and 30) which is my pride and joy. Most saucepan manufacturers include a steamer assembly in their range of pans. There are even electric steamers. If, like me, you've shied away from buying a microwave—don't. Many steamed dishes can be microwaved: just adapt the cooking times according to the manufacturer's instructions.

The recipes in this book are inspired by East and Southeast Asian cuisines, but, when you've started steaming, you'll discover many more. My own passion is for the steamed foods of India—but that's another book!

Boiled or char-grilled corn is ubiquitous street food all over Asia. In some places, I've seen it boiled within an inch of its life so all the kernels are blown out. It's then brushed with butter, char-grilled for the customers, then topped with a large dash of chile powder for the bravest souls. Serve this steamed version with Chinese spiced salt or Vietnamese nuòc cham—or both.

Chile Corn with Spiced Salt

6 ears of corn

2 limes, cut into wedges, to serve

Chinese Spiced Salt

½ tablespoon red peppercorns

½ tablespoon white peppercorns

½ tablespoon green peppercorns

½ tablespoon black peppercorns

½ tablespoon Szechuan peppercorns or, if unavailable, extra black peppercorns

3 tablespoons sea salt flakes

Nuòc Cham Dipping Sauce

1 garlic clove, crushed

1 red bird's eye chile, finely sliced

2 tablespoons sugar

½ lime

¼ cup fish sauce

Serves 6

To make the Chinese spiced salt, put the peppercorns into a dry skillet and heat gently to release the aromas. Transfer to a blender and blend until coarsely crushed. Alternatively, use a mortar and pestle. Stir in the salt and transfer to a small serving bowl.

To make the nuòc cham dipping sauce, grind the garlic, chile, and sugar with a mortar and pestle to form a paste. Stir in the lime juice, fish sauce, and 3 tablespoons water. Transfer to a small serving bowl.

To prepare the corn, remove the husks and silks, if any. Cut the ears crosswise into ¾-inch chunks. Steam until tender, then serve with lime wedges, the spiced salt, and/or the nuòc cham dipping sauce.

1 lb. shelled soy beans, fresh or
frozen, or 1½ lb. in the pod

Peanut Sambal

¼ cup peanut butter
or 1 cup roasted peanuts

1 onion, finely chopped

2 large garlic cloves, crushed

1–2 medium hot red chiles, such
as serrano, seeded and chopped

1 tablespoon fish sauce

grated zest of 1 lime,
preferably kaffir lime, plus freshly
squeezed lime juice, to taste

1 inch fresh ginger,
peeled and grated

3 tablespoons peanut oil

2 tablespoons brown sugar

½ cup coconut cream
(see note page 57)

To serve

2 scallions, halved,
then finely sliced lengthwise

½ red pepper or 1 red chile,
such as bird's eye, seeded
and finely sliced lengthwise

1 tablespoon peanuts,
coarsely chopped

Serves 4

**A New York friend has a passion for fresh soy
beans—endamame—so this recipe is for her.
They are available in Chinese stores and
some supermarkets. I've put them together
with an easy, all-purpose sambal, the spicy
condiment native to Indonesia and Malaysia.**

Fresh Soy Beans
with Peanut Sambal

To make the sambal, put the peanut butter or peanuts,
onion, garlic, chiles, fish sauce, lime zest, and ginger
into a small food processor and grind to a paste.
Alternatively, use a mortar and pestle.

Put the oil into a small skillet or wok, add the paste
and sugar, and stir-fry for 2 minutes to release the
flavors. Add the coconut milk and simmer gently until
the oil comes to the surface. Do not let boil. Add lime
juice to taste.

Put the soy beans, shelled or whole, onto a plate in a
steamer and steam until tender. Transfer to a serving
plate and spoon the sambal on top (loosen with a little
hot water if the paste is too thick). Top the beans with
the scallions. Add a few crushed peanuts and sliced
pepper or chile, then serve. The sambal may also be
served in a small bowl.

I make this recipe with the tiny peppers, about 2 inches long, sold in supermarkets. They make excellent two-bite-size fingerfood for parties. If you can't find baby bell peppers, use larger ones and cut them in half crosswise. You could also use very mild, largish chile peppers, but they mustn't be too spicy, and you should leave the curry paste out of the filling.

Baby Bell Peppers with Chile Peanuts

1 lb. baby bell peppers

Chile Peanut Filling

1 bundle beanthread vermicelli noodles, about 1 oz.*

4 oz. roasted salted peanuts, about ¾ cup

1 tablespoon red Thai curry paste

1 garlic clove, crushed

grated zest and juice of 1 lime

1 tablespoon sugar

1 tablespoon sesame oil

Serves 4–8

Using a sharp knife, cut the top off each bell pepper and scoop out the seeds and membranes.

To prepare the filling, put the noodles into a bowl, cover with hot water and set aside for 15 minutes. Drain and chop coarsely with kitchen shears.

Put the peanuts into a skillet and dry-toast until aromatic, about 30 seconds. Put into a small blender, add the curry paste, garlic, lime zest and juice, sugar, and sesame oil, and grind to a paste. Alternatively, use a mortar and pestle.

Stuff the peppers with the peanut mixture, alternately with the noodles, using your fingers to mix the two inside the peppers. (Do not stuff too tightly.) Put the peppers, open side up, into a small bamboo steamer, then put it inside a larger steamer. Steam for about 30 minutes, or until the peppers are tender. Serve in the small steamer, with other Asian dishes.

*Note Beanthread noodles (also known as cellophane or glass noodles) are available loose, or in small bundles, about 1 oz. each.

8 baby zucchini or pattypans, green or yellow, halved lengthwise

4 Chinese yard-long beans, cut into 4-inch lengths (optional)

3 oz. green beans, stalks trimmed, points not

4 oz. shelled green peas, fresh or frozen, about 1 cup

12 small asparagus tips

3 oz. sugar snap peas

3 oz. snowpeas, halved lengthwise (optional)

Lemon Soy Butter

1 stick unsalted butter

6 scallions, sliced crosswise

1 inch fresh ginger, peeled and grated

1 teaspoon Japanese seven-spice (shichimi togarishi) or freshly ground black pepper

½ cup sake

freshly squeezed juice of 1–1½ lemons, about ½ cup

2 tablespoons Japanese soy sauce (shoyu)

Serves 4

Green vegetables, such as peas and beans, love steam and stay deliciously crunchy. Use any combination, according to what's available that day. Butter isn't a traditional ingredient in East and Southeast Asia, but is now seen more and more. With lemon and soy, it makes a delicious dressing—for Western dishes too.

Green Vegetables with Lemon Soy Butter

To make the lemon soy butter, put the butter into a saucepan, add the scallions, ginger, seven-spice, sake, lemon juice, and soy sauce, and heat gently. Set aside, but keep the mixture warm.

Put a steamer over boiling water, add the zucchini first and steam for about 1 minute. Add both kinds of beans and the asparagus and steam until all are tender but crisp. As each vegetable is done, transfer to a bowl of ice water to stop it cooking further.

Put the shelled peas into a small, heatproof bowl and add to the steamer. Add the sugar snaps and snowpeas and steam until just tender—as each is done, transfer to the bowl of ice water.

When all are done, drain in a colander, then put the colander into the steamer to reheat the vegetables, about 2 minutes. Transfer to a heated serving dish, pour over the lemon soy butter, and serve as an accompaniment for other dishes.

Chinese Greens
with Star Anise Butter

Steaming is the perfect way to cook most leafy greens. They keep their nutrients and bright color and need just a sprinkle of sauce to give them spark. Use simple oyster or mushroom sauces—or one of my favorites, butter flavored with whole star anise.

1 lb. Asian greens such as Chinese broccoli, Chinese flowering cabbage or mustard cabbage, choi sum or baby bok choy, broccoli rabe or broccoli florets, or napa cabbage or regular cabbage, thickly sliced

Anise Butter

3 whole star anise

1 stick unsalted butter

½ teaspoon soy sauce, or to taste

1 tablespoon sesame oil

6 scallions, trimmed and sliced crosswise

Serves 4

Steam the chosen greens until just tender. Choy sum and bok choy will take about 4 minutes, or until the leaves are just wilted and the stems tender (take care not to overcook). Broccoli will take a few minutes longer.

Meanwhile, put the star anise into small saucepan, add the butter, soy sauce, sesame oil, and scallions and melt over low heat. Alternatively, put into a bowl and microwave on HIGH for about 30 seconds. Set aside to infuse while the greens finish cooking.

To serve, transfer the greens to a plate, reheat the dressing, pour over the greens and serve.

Note If you're using any member of the cabbage family, don't cook it for more than about 7 minutes. After that time, it develops that infamous cabbagy smell. In any case, it will taste much nicer if it's still crunchy.

Japanese Oysters
with Mirin and Ginger

Oysters can be big or little, according to where you live, but I think only large, assertively flavored oysters should be used for cooking. Use 3–5 per person, depending on size (I think even numbers are unlucky, and you can't tempt fate with oysters!) You can change the emphasis of this dish with different flavorings: try lime zest, lemongrass, and ginger for a Southeast Asian taste.

3–5 oysters per person, depending on size

4 scallions

sea salt flakes, for serving

1 tablespoon Japanese pickled ginger, finely sliced

Mirin and Ginger Sauce

½ cup mirin (rice wine)

3 tablespoons white rice vinegar

3 tablespoons Japanese soy sauce (shoyu), or fish sauce for a Southeast Asian flavor

1 inch fresh ginger, peeled and finely chopped

4 scallions, finely sliced

Serves 4

Open the oysters, or get the fish seller to do it for you. If the latter, make sure this is done a very short time before you steam them.

Trim the scallions, halve them crosswise into white and green, then finely slice lengthwise.

To make the sauce, put the mirin, vinegar, soy sauce, ginger, and scallions into a small saucepan and stir over a low heat until just warm.

Put the oysters onto a plate in a steamer (if the oysters are large, you may have to use several layers). Spoon 1 teaspoon of the dressing into each one.

Put the lid on the steamer and steam for about 2 minutes. Remove the lid and turn off the heat. Serve the oysters on a bed of sea salt flakes, and sprinkle with the scallion and pickled ginger.

Note Remember, you aren't cooking the oysters, merely heating them. If you cook them, they'll shrink— just heat them, and you'll develop their flavors.

4 lb. mussels, washed, scrubbed
and debearded, or clams,
or a mixture of both

1 inch fresh ginger or galangal,
peeled and chopped

2 stalks of lemongrass, trimmed,
peeled, and finely sliced

a handful of cilantro, plus the
roots if available, chopped

2 kaffir lime leaves,
very finely shredded crosswise,
or the grated zest of 1 lime

a handful Thai basil leaves
(optional), torn

2–4 red bird's eye chiles

3 garlic cloves, crushed

5 Thai pink shallots or
1 regular, sliced

1 cup fish stock

3 tablespoons fish sauce

juice of 1 lime

Chile Dipping Sauce

juice of 1 lime

3 tablespoons fish sauce

1–2 red bird's eye chiles, crushed

2 garlic cloves, crushed

2 teaspoons sugar

Serves 4

These mussels glory under the name of *hoy mang poo*. I love the name so much I had to include a recipe. Mussels and clams are perfectly designed for eating with chopsticks.

Spicy Hot Mussels

Check the mussels by tapping each one against a work surface. They should close tightly—discard any that remain open. Scrub the shells with a small brush and remove the wiry beards. Rinse and transfer to bowls and arrange in one or more layers of a steamer—the bowls should be deep enough to catch all the juices the mussels produce.

Put the ginger, lemongrass, cilantro, lime leaves, and basil, if using, into a small food processor and work to a paste. Add the chiles, garlic, and shallots and blend again. Alternatively, use a mortar and pestle. Stir in the stock, fish sauce, and lime juice, then pour over the mussels.

Steam until the mussels open, discarding any that fail to open.

To make the dipping sauce, put the lime juice, fish sauce, chiles, garlic, and sugar into a bowl. Mix well, then divide between 4 small dipping bowls and serve with the mussels.

Steamed Shrimp Stuffed with Chile

Southeast Asian chile pastes are some of my favorite spicy mixtures—complex and delicious. You'll need lots of hot towels to mop up spicy fingers after eating this hands-on dish.

3–5 shrimp per person, depending on size, unpeeled and uncooked

¼ cup mirin, Shaohsing (rice wine), or dry sherry

freshly squeezed juice of 1 lime, plus 3 extra limes, halved, to serve

Chile Jam

4 oz. dried shrimp

8 garlic cloves, unpeeled

10 Thai pink shallots or 2 regular

2 tablespoons peanut oil

12 large dried red chiles, medium hot, broken in half and seeded

1 tablespoon tamarind paste

2 tablespoons brown sugar

1 tablespoon fish sauce

Serves 4

To make the chile jam, put the dried shrimp onto a piece of aluminum foil and crumple up the edges. Put onto a baking tray. Add the garlic and shallots and transfer to a preheated oven and cook at 400°F until dark brown and aromatic, about 30 minutes. Remove the shrimp on their sheet of foil after 10 minutes.

Put 1 tablespoon of the oil into a small skillet, add the chiles, and stir-fry for a few seconds to release the aromas. Grind to a meal with a mortar and pestle or in a blender, then add the shrimp and grind again. Add the garlic and shallots and grind again. Put the tamarind paste into a small bowl and stir in 2 tablespoons water, the sugar, and fish sauce.

Add the remaining 1 tablespoon oil to the skillet, add the chile mixture, and heat until aromatic. Stir in the tamarind mixture and cook until thick. Set aside until cool enough to handle. Store any leftover mixture in the refrigerator for up to 3 days (it can be used as stuffing for the recipes on pages 13 and 27, with stir-fried scallops, or even grilled steak).

Cut down the backs of the unshelled shrimp and remove the vein. Press the chile jam into the back cut, pushing it between the shell and flesh as much as possible. Put onto a plate in a steamer, sprinkle with mirin and lime juice, and steam just until opaque. Do not overcook or the shrimp will be tough. Serve with lime halves and hot towels.

Where I grew up, the crabs were enormous, with armory that was purported to be able to snip your finger off and flesh that was truly delectable. They are, however, becoming somewhat expensive these days—and smaller. There was another variety, the pretty Blue Swimmer, which I prefer for this dish. Use whatever crabs are popular where you live. Steaming is a delicious way to prepare crabs—they don't become watery, as they sometimes do when boiled.

Blue Swimmer Crabs
with Chile, Lime, and Ginger

4–8 swimmer crabs or other small crabs, depending on size, or 2 larger crabs

6 scallions, sliced

Lime and Ginger Dressing

¼ cup peanut oil

¼ cup mirin (rice wine)

2 inches fresh ginger, finely sliced

freshly squeezed juice of 2 limes, lime halves reserved

2 teaspoons sugar

2 tablespoons fish sauce

2 medium red chiles, finely sliced

Serves 4

To make the dressing, heat the oil in a wok or small saucepan, add the mirin, ginger, lime juice, sugar, fish sauce, and chiles, and and stir-fry for about 1 minute. Add 1 tablespoon water and the squeezed lime halves, and cook for a further 1 minute. Remove from the heat until the crabs are ready.

Put the crabs into a steamer and steam until they have turned red. Remove from the steamer, let cool a little, then pry off the shells and remove the feathery sections from the bodies. Break or cut the bodies into 2, 4, or 8, depending on size, then put the bodies and top shells into the wok.

Stir-fry briskly to coat with the sauce, then toss the sliced scallions over the top. Transfer to a serving platter and serve with crab picks or chopsticks to push out the flesh, plus hot towels for wiping your hands later.

Some of the ingredients for this stuffing—lemongrass, chile paste, lime leaves, kaffir limes, and grated ginger—can be frozen and used from frozen. The squid usually have their pink skins rubbed off: try leaving it on—it looks pretty and tastes wonderful.

Steamed Stuffed Baby Squid

1 lb. baby squid, about
2–3 inches long, thawed if frozen

Stuffing

3 kaffir lime leaves

3 stalks of lemongrass

1 kaffir lime, preferably frozen
(to make the flesh easier to grate)

2 teaspoons green Thai curry paste

1 shallot, chopped

1 garlic clove, crushed

1 inch fresh ginger,
peeled and grated

2 tablespoons mirin, Shaohsing
(rice wine), or dry sherry

2 tablespoons fish sauce

peanut or canola oil, for cooking

2 hot Italian pork sausages

1 bundle beanthread noodles,
about 1 oz. (see note, page 13)

Serves 4

To clean the squid, pull the tentacles out of the bodies, cut off and chop the tentacles, and reserve them. Remove and discard the transparent quill and rinse out the bodies.

To make the stuffing, cut the central vein out of the kaffir lime leaves and very finely chop the remainder. Remove the outer leaves of the lemongrass, finely slice the lower 2 inches of each stalk, and discard the rest.

Finely grate the kaffir lime zest. Cut off and discard the white pith, then grate half the lime, either refreezing or discarding the remainder. Put the curry paste, shallot, garlic, and ginger into a bowl, then stir in the lime zest and grated lime, lime leaves, lemongrass, mirin, and fish sauce.

Put the noodles into a second bowl and cover with hot water. Set aside for 15 minutes, then drain and cover with cold water. Just before using, drain again and chop into short sections with kitchen shears.

Scrape the pork meat out of the sausages, discarding the skins. Add the meat to the bowl of stuffing. Using a hand-held stick blender, work to a paste. Heat 2 tablespoons oil in a skillet or wok and stir-fry the mixture until the pork is cooked and dried out, about 5 minutes. Transfer to a bowl and put the bowl into a pan of cold water to cool quickly. When cool, stir in the noodles and chopped tentacles.

Fill each squid body with the pork and noodle mixture. Use your fingers, or a bottle filling funnel and a chopstick as a pusher. As each body is filled, secure it with a toothpick. If serving as finger food, put another toothpick through the other end too. Arrange in a single layer in a steamer, then steam for 10 minutes, and serve. If using as fingerfood, cut in half before serving.

1 salmon fillet, about 1–1½ lb.

salt

1 bundle soba buckwheat noodles, about 4 oz.

1 bundle green tea noodles (cha-somen), about 4 oz.

1 sheet kombu seaweed, wiped with a cloth, then cut into 4 pieces (optional)*

¼ cup sake

Dashi Sauce

1 cup dashi stock

¾ cup mirin (rice wine)

¾ cup Japanese soy sauce (shoyu)

a handful of dried bonito flakes (optional)

Serves 4

Cut the salmon crosswise into 4 strips and put the pieces, skin side down, onto a plate sprinkled with a layer of salt. Set aside for 20 minutes, then rinse off the salt and pat dry with paper towels.

Bring a large saucepan of water to a boil, add the noodles, and cook, stirring a little with chopsticks, until the water returns to a boil. Add a splash of cold water and return to a boil. Repeat this 2 more times, until the noodles are *al dente*—a total of 3–4 minutes. Drain, rinse in cold water, and set aside.

When ready to assemble, dip the noodles into boiling water and drain. Put pieces of kombu seaweed, if using, into 4 lidded ceramic bowls (alternatively, use bowls with a small saucer as a lid). Add a pile of noodles and top with a fish fillet, skin side up.

Sprinkle 1 tablespoon sake over each one, put a circle of foil on top and the lid on top of that. Put the bowls into one or more tiers of a bamboo steamer. Steam for about 10 minutes or until the fish is cooked, but still pink in the middle.

Put the dashi sauce ingredients into a saucepan, bring to the boil, and, when ready to serve, strain over the fish. Serve with chopsticks and small spoons. Heavenly!

*Note The kombu seaweed is there for flavor— discard before eating.

This is a very elegant and stylish dish, and easy to make—the bowls can be assembled beforehand, then cooked at the very last minute. The traditional Japanese practice of salting the fish increases the succulence of its flesh when cooked—a great secret for all fish cooks!

Japanese Steamed Fish
on Noodles with Seaweed

Banana leaves are the traditional wraps for this famous dish from Malaysia, but you could also use foil or even wax paper. Use a firm fish—though Malaysia doesn't have salmon, I use this because it's widely available and marries well with spicy flavors. I warn you—this one's hot! If you want something slightly less fiery, use fewer chiles.

Otak Otak Fish Packages

1¼ lb. firm fish without bones, such as salmon, mackerel, or cod

3 teaspoons salt

4 eggs

3 kaffir lime leaves, central stems removed and remainder finely sliced

1 cup coconut cream (see note page 57)

banana leaves or foil, for wrapping

Chile Paste

5 small dried chiles, soaked in boiling water for 15 minutes

5 red bird's eye chiles, chopped

5 Thai pink shallots or 1 regular

2 garlic cloves, crushed

2 stalks of lemongrass, trimmed, peeled, and finely sliced

1 inch fresh ginger, peeled and sliced

1 tablespoon fish sauce

1 teaspoon ground turmeric

Makes 20

Cut the fish into pieces 1 x 2 inches, sprinkle with 1 teaspoon of the salt, and set aside for 15 minutes.

To make the chile paste, drain the soaked chiles and put into a small blender. Add the bird's eye chiles, shallots, garlic, lemongrass, ginger, fish sauce, and turmeric and blend well. Alternatively, use a mortar and pestle.

Put the eggs into a bowl and beat lightly with a fork. Add the chile paste and lime leaves and stir well. Stir in the coconut cream and 1 teaspoon of the salt.

Wash and dry the banana leaves, if using. Warm them over an open flame for a few seconds until softened, then cut into pieces about 6 x 8 inches.

Put a piece of fish in the center of each piece of leaf. Bring the 2 long sides together, then fold one of the short sides so the middle meets the 2 long edges. Fold the wings back and keep together (I use a paperclip or plastic clothes peg). Add about 2 tablespoons of the egg mixture to the package and fold the other end in the same way. Fasten with a long toothpick or piece of bamboo skewer. You can also trim the top with kitchen shears to make a neat package.

Steam for 20 minutes, then serve with other Asian dishes.

Spicy Salmon Pots

Steamed in small ceramic bowls, this spicy salmon dish is based on an original using banana leaf cups. Instead of the banana leaf, I have used strips of pandanus—a delicious ingredient that adds scent and pretty green color to some Southeast Asian dishes. Omit if unavailable.

1 egg, beaten

1½ cups thick coconut cream (see note page 57)

1 tablespoon rice flour

1 lb. salmon or other fish fillets, sliced crosswise into fine strips

1–3 red bird's eye chiles, seeded and finely sliced, plus extra to serve

2 tablespoons Thai green curry paste

1½ tablespoons fish sauce

2 scallions, finely sliced

4 pandanus leaves* (optional)

4 kaffir lime leaves, bruised with a fork

4 small bowls or ramekins, greased with peanut oil

Serves 4

Put the egg into a mixing bowl, add the coconut cream and rice flour, and beat well. Reserve ¼ cup of the mixture.

Add the strips of fish to the mixing bowl, then stir in the chiles, curry paste, fish sauce, and scallions.

Line the greased small bowls or ramekins with strips of pandanus leaf, if using.

Divide half the fish mixture between the small bowls or ramekins and put into one or more tiers of a steamer. Wrap the lid of the steamer in a cloth to stop the condensation dropping back into the bowls. Steam for 7 minutes, then divide the remaining fish mixture between the bowls. Add a lime leaf to each, then pour over the reserved ¼ cup of the coconut cream mixture.

Steam until firm, then serve, topped with a few slices of chile.

This dish can also be microwaved. Cook, covered, on MEDIUM for 10 minutes, then cook on HIGH, uncovered, for 5 minutes.

*Note Pandanus, kewra, or screwpine leaves are found in Asian markets. Indian stores sometimes have kewra water—add just a drop to the coconut cream mixture to appreciate the scent.

Chinese Steamed Fish

Chinese cooks are very discerning in choosing their fish—they like a fine-textured fish with good flavor for this dish. I used a beautiful red grouper, but red snapper is also good. Remember to take the lid of the steamer with you when you buy the fish to make sure it will fit.

4–5 Chinese dried mushrooms

1 bundle beanthread vermicelli noodles, about 1 oz. (see note page 13)

1 large whole fish, such as grouper or snapper, about 2 lb., cleaned and scaled

salt

2 inches fresh ginger, peeled and very finely sliced

3 garlic cloves, crushed

6 scallions, finely sliced lengthwise

1 tablespoon peanut oil, for brushing

2 tablespoons soy sauce or fish sauce

1 teaspoon sugar

2 tablespoons Shaohsing, mirin (rice wine), or dry sherry

1 oval serving plate, to fit inside the steamer

Serves 4

Put the mushrooms into a bowl, cover with boiling water, and let soak for 15 minutes. Drain, remove the stems if any, then roughly slice the caps.

Put the serving plate into a large steamer. Put the dried noodles onto the plate, then add the sliced mushrooms.

Rinse the fish in salted water, then pat dry with paper towels. Stuff the cavity with the ginger, garlic, and half the scallions, then brush the skin with the oil. Blanch the remaining scallions in boiling water for 10 seconds, then drain.

Put the fish onto the oval plate on top of the noodles and mushrooms. Put the soy sauce, sugar, and Shaohsing into a bowl, mix quickly, then sprinkle over the fish.

Put the steamer into a wok about one-third full of boiling water. Steam until the flesh has become opaque (the time will depend on the thickness of the fish, but about 20–30 minutes is usual). Add extra boiling water as necessary.

Remove the steamer from the wok, then remove the plate from the steamer. Wipe the underside dry with paper towels.

Top with the blanched scallions and serve. (I always discard the flavorings from the cavity before serving, but leave the noodles and mushrooms, which will soak up lots of flavor from the juices.)

Note It is regarded as bad luck to turn the fish over. Serve it from one side of the bone, then remove and discard the bones and serve the rest of the fish. You can also debone the fish before serving, reassembling it carefully on the plate.

Savory custards are found all over East and Southeast Asia—I give two versions here. Ingredients can vary according to what's available, but, if you include meat or poultry, it should be cooked first.

Steamed Japanese Custard

1 chicken breast, brushed with soy sauce

about 20 small peeled shrimp, preferably uncooked

1 thick trout fillet, about 12 inches long, cut into 1-inch pieces

a handful of dried black fungus, soaked in boiling water for 15 minutes, then drained

a large handful of honigiri or enokitake mushrooms, roots trimmed

6 scallions, the white and all the green, sliced diagonally

1 carrot, finely sliced with a vegetable peeler, then sliced into strips

6 eggs

Dashi Mixture

1 tablespoon Japanese soy sauce (shoyu)

1 tablespoon mirin (rice wine)

1 cup dashi stock, made from instant dashi-bonito stock powder

Serves 4

To make the dashi mixture, put the soy sauce, mirin, and made-up dashi stock into a saucepan and heat gently. Remove from the heat and plunge the pan into cold water to cool down the mixture as quickly as possible.

Meanwhile, put the chicken breast into a steamer and steam for about 15 minutes or until cooked through. Remove and pull into shreds. Divide between 4 bowls. Add a share of the shrimp, trout, drained fungus (sliced into smaller pieces if necessary), honigiri or enokitake mushrooms, scallions, and carrot strips.

Beat the eggs and strain them into a bowl, then stir in the cooled dashi mixture. Pour into the bowls, filling almost to the top, making sure some of the ingredients show through the surface. Cover with foil and put into a steamer for about 15 minutes. To test, remove the foil and press with your finger—the surface should be firm but yielding. If still liquid, steam for a few minutes longer until set.

Serve in the bowls with small Chinese spoons.

Variation To make a Southeast Asian version, instead of the dashi mixture, put 1 cup coconut milk into a saucepan. Add 1 teaspoon Thai red chile paste, 1 tablespoon fish sauce, 1 teaspoon chile oil, and 1 tablespoon mirin. Heat gently to blend the flavors, then cool as quickly as possible. Proceed as in the main recipe. This version will take about 5–10 minutes longer to cook. Serve topped with sliced chiles and grated lime zest.

Chicken & Meat

In Southeast Asia, small birds are stuffed with various flavorings, then steamed. A Cornish hen will serve one person. For the quail variation, allow two birds each. This is a good way to spice up their rather bland flavor.

4 Cornish hens

4 limes, sliced into wedges, plus extra to serve

4 inches fresh ginger, sliced

8 star anise

¼ cup honey

½ cup mirin, Shaohsing (rice wine), or dry sherry

2 tablespoons sesame oil

¼ cup fish sauce

8 scallions, halved lengthwise, then crosswise

8 Chinese dried mushrooms, soaked in boiling water for 15 minutes

4 small bowls, just big enough to fit the hens

Serves 4

Cornish Hens Stuffed with Lime and Ginger

Stuff each Cornish hen with a share of the lime wedges, sliced ginger, and 4 of the star anise. Truss with kitchen twine.

Put the honey into a bowl and stir in the mirin, sesame oil, fish sauce, scallions, and remaining star anise. Drain the mushrooms, cut into strips, then add to the bowl. Stir to dissolve the honey.

Divide the mixture between the 4 bowls, add the hens, and turn to coat with the liquid. Steam the birds, breast down, for 45 minutes or until tender, turning them over twice during the cooking time. Top up with boiling water as needed. Serve in the bowls.

Variation **Ginger Quail** Heat 2 tablespoons peanut oil in a skillet, add 4 oz. diced pancetta, 1 chopped shallot, 4 crushed garlic cloves, and 2 tablespoons grated ginger. Stir-fry until crisp and golden—do not let the garlic burn. Taste and add fish sauce or a pinch of salt if needed. Let cool a little, then use to stuff 8 quail. Put each quail onto a sheet of foil or banana leaf and spoon 1 tablespoon thick coconut cream (see note page 57) over each one. Wrap up the packages, scrunching up the foil or securing the leaves with a toothpick. Steam for about 45 minutes to 1 hour, or until done. Open the packages and serve on a platter.

An easy, delicious, and quick dish to prepare when you come home from work, dog-tired. It takes all of 5 minutes to prepare and about 10 minutes to cook—quicker than most supermarket meals. Vary the vegetables according to what's in the refrigerator.

Steamed Chicken over Rice

1 chicken breast

3 scallions

1 garlic clove, crushed

1 inch fresh ginger, peeled and grated

2 tablespoons oyster sauce

2 tablespoons mirin, Shaohsing (rice wine), or dry sherry

1 red or yellow bell pepper, peeled, seeded, and sliced

a handful of asparagus tips, chopped into 1-inch lengths

1 cup fragrant Thai rice or jasmine rice

soy sauce, to serve

Serves 1

Cut the chicken into ½-inch slices lengthwise. Put into a small bowl just big enough fit into a saucepan, leaving about 1 inch all round.

Chop the scallions into ½-inch pieces and add to the chicken. Add the garlic and grated ginger, oyster sauce, mirin, sliced bell pepper, and asparagus and turn to coat with the mixture. Set aside for 30 minutes to develop the flavors if time allows.

Put the rice into the saucepan and add enough water to come one-and-a-half finger's joints above the rice. Push the rice aside, leaving a bare circle in the middle. Put the bowl of chicken into the saucepan, with the base in the hole. Put the lid on the saucepan, bring to a boil, reduce the heat, and simmer for about 12 minutes. Turn off the heat and set aside for 10 minutes without lifting the lid. By this time, the rice should be fluffy and dry and the chicken tender. Serve with soy sauce.

Grated Ginger Many recipes call for just 1 inch of ginger, peeled and grated, yet it's only ever sold in huge rhizomes. My answer is to break the root into pieces and let soak in water for about 15 minutes (this is to refresh the root, which will have dried out somewhat since it was picked). Peel with a vegetable peeler, then put into a small blender or food processor and blend to a purée, adding a little water if necessary. Spoon the purée into ice cube trays, freeze, then transfer to a plastic bag. Voila! You have a cube of grated ginger—about 1 inch—whenever you need it.

You would need a super-size steamer to fit a whole duck. I usually solve the space problem by cutting off the wings and keeping them for stock, and either steaming the legs separately or using them for another recipe.

Cilantro Ginger Duck Salad

a large bunch of cilantro

3 inches fresh ginger, sliced

3 garlic cloves, crushed

1 duck, legs and wings removed

½ cup mirin, Shaohsing (rice wine), or dry sherry

½ cup dark soy sauce

2 tablespoons sesame oil

2 tablespoons honey

grated zest of 1 lemon

To serve

2 bundles beanthread noodles, 1 oz. each (see note page 30)

about 8 oz. mixed salad leaves

a handful of salted peanuts, toasted in a dry skillet

a few sprigs of cilantro

2–3 scallions, sliced lengthwise

Serves 4

Wash the cilantro well, then put it into a bowl with the ginger and garlic. Mix well, then stuff into the duck cavity. Put the duck onto a large, double sheet of foil, large enough to enclose it completely. Fold the foil along the top and scrunch it closed. Fold and scrunch one end of the package closed.

Put a second double sheet of foil running the opposite way and scrunch closed at the sides, still keeping the end open. Put the duck, breast side down, into a large steamer with the open end upwards.

Put the mirin, soy sauce, sesame oil, honey, and lemon zest into a saucepan and heat to dissolve the honey. Pour half the mixture into the package and scrunch the foil closed, making sure no liquid runs out. Reserve the remainder.

Steam over a large saucepan of water for about 1½ hours, topping up with extra boiling water as necessary. Unwrap after 1 hour and test. The duck can be slightly rare. Remove the duck from the steamer and let rest for about 10 minutes. Unwrap the foil, and drain off and discard the liquid. Shred the meat from the duck and keep it warm.

Soak the noodles in hot water for 15 minutes, then drain and plunge into cold water. Drain, then toss in the reserved mirin mixture.

Arrange salad leaves on 4 plates, then add the cold noodles and shredded duck. Sprinkle with the toasted peanuts, sprigs of cilantro, and scallions. Spoon the remaining dressing from the noodles over the top and serve.

If you live near a Chinatown market, you can buy their delicious grilled pork. If you don't, try the home-style version I give below, reserving a little for the buns.

Steamed Pork Buns

1 tablespoon peanut oil

1 tablespoon chopped onion

1 garlic clove, crushed

4 oz. Chinese grilled pork, finely chopped*

2 scallions, chopped

1 teaspoon soy sauce

freshly ground black pepper

½ teaspoon sugar

¼ teaspoon sesame oil

Bun Dough

2½ cups all-purpose flour

2½ teaspoons baking powder

1 tablespoon sugar

½ teaspoon salt

1 tablespoon peanut oil

¼ teaspoon sesame oil

8 pieces of wax paper, 4 inches square

Makes 8

Heat the oil in a wok, add the onion and garlic, and stir-fry until golden. Add the pork, scallions, soy sauce, pepper, sugar, and sesame oil, stir-fry quickly at high heat, then reduce the heat and simmer gently for about 5 minutes. Let cool.

To make the dough, sift the flour and baking powder into a bowl, then stir in the sugar and salt. Stir in the peanut and sesame oils and knead to form a soft dough. Cover and set aside for 1 hour.

Turn out the dough onto a work surface and knead for 5 minutes. Divide into 8, then roll each piece of dough into a ball and flatten to a disk. Divide the filling into 8 portions, then put 1 portion the middle of each disk. Gradually work the outside edge of the disk around and over the top to enclose the filling. Seal.

Put 8 pieces of wax paper into one or more tiers of a steamer. Brush the paper with oil. Put the buns, sealed side down and well apart, onto the pieces of paper. Steam over simmering water for about 30 minutes, until well puffed, then serve.

*Chinese Grilled Pork Cut 2 lb. pork tenderloin into two long strips lengthwise. Rub with 1 tablespoon pepper and 1 tablespoon Chinese five-spice powder. Put ¼ cup soy sauce into a shallow dish and stir in 2 teaspoons sesame oil. Add the pork and turn to coat well. Cover and chill overnight to develop the flavors. Next day, return to room temperature for 1 hour, then cook on an outdoor grill or roast on a rack in a preheated oven at 400°F for 15 minutes. Reduce the heat to 350°F and continue roasting for another 20 minutes. Let rest for 20 minutes before cutting.

The round dumpling wrappers for this variation of a Cantonese classic are available in the refrigerator sections of Chinese supermarkets. You can also use wonton wrappers, but they won't have the perfect, moon-white translucence of the real thing. Dim sum make great party food: cook and serve in Chinese spoons or on plates a little smaller than the steamer.

Dim Sum with Pepper Soy

6 Chinese dried mushrooms

4 oz. cooked, peeled red shrimp

6 oz. bacon

4 oz. skinless chicken breast

1 tablespoon cornstarch

1 tablespoon peanut oil

10 water chestnuts, finely diced

1 tablespoon mirin, Shaohsing (rice wine), or dry sherry

1 teaspoon sugar

1 teaspoon sesame oil

1½ tablespoons dark soy sauce

1 inch fresh ginger, peeled and grated

2 packages dumpling wrappers

single leaves of cilantro

To serve

½ cup soy sauce

1 tablespoon Japanese seven-spice (shichimi togarishi)

Makes about 50

Put the mushrooms into a bowl and cover with boiling water for about 15 minutes to rehydrate. Drain and squeeze as dry as possible. Remove the stems and any hard pieces. Chop the mushrooms finely and put into a bowl.

Split the shrimp in half lengthwise, then into ¾-inch-long pieces. Reserve.

Chop the bacon and chicken and transfer to a small food processor. Add the cornstarch and blend to a paste.

Put the oil into a wok and heat well, swirling the oil around the surface. Add the chicken paste and stir-fry, breaking up any lumps, until opaque. Add the mushrooms, water chestnuts, mirin, sugar, sesame oil, soy sauce, and grated ginger. Stir-fry until heated through, to mix the flavors, then let cool and chill.

When ready to assemble, working on 2–3 wrappers at a time and keeping the others covered, put 1 heaping teaspoon of the chicken mixture in the center. Put a piece of shrimp, red side out, on one side of the filling, and a cilantro leaf on the other side. Dip your finger in water and run it around the edge of the wrapper. Bring the edges of the wrapper together to form a half moon, then pleat the edges to form a crest. Tap the base of the moon on the work surface to flatten. Cover with a cloth until all the dumplings have been made.

Arrange apart on small serving plates or Chinese spoons (brushed with oil) to fit inside one or more tiers of a steamer. Steam for 9–10 minutes until done— the dough will become slightly translucent, letting the green cilantro and red shrimp show through. Serve with a simple dip of soy sauce and seven-spice.

Food writer Clare Ferguson serves a chicken version of these moneybags at parties. She cooks them in bamboo steamers, then serves them still in the steamers. If you cook three tiers at a time, you can serve the first batch while the next one is cooking. The bacon isn't traditional, but it means you need less salt.

Wonton Pork Moneybags

1 lb. ground pork

4 oz. shelled shrimp

3 slices bacon, chopped

1 teaspoon crushed pepper, preferably Szechuan

1 egg white

2 teaspoons sesame oil

1 inch fresh ginger, peeled and grated

2 teaspoons salt

1 garlic clove, crushed

2 teaspoons cornstarch

4 scallions

4 canned water chestnuts, finely diced

1 Chinese yard-long bean or 4 green beans, finely sliced

1–2 packages wonton wrappers*

banana leaves or parchment paper, for steaming

soy sauce, to serve

Serves 10

Put the pork, shrimp, and bacon into a food processor and blend to a purée. With the motor running, add the pepper, egg white, sesame oil, ginger, salt, garlic, and cornstarch.

Finely chop the white and green parts of the scallions crosswise, transfer to a mixing bowl, then add the pork mixture, water chestnuts, and bean(s). Mix well—using your hands is the most efficient way.

Cut the square wonton wrappers into rounds with kitchen shears—keep them covered with a cloth so they don't dry out. Put about 1 tablespoon of the pork filling in the center of each round wrapper. Use a teaspoon to smooth the mixture almost to the edges.

Cup the wonton in the palm of your hand. Gather up your hand, pushing down with the teaspoon: you will achieve an open-topped, pleated, money-bag-shaped container filled with mixture. Drop it gently onto a floured work surface to flatten the bottom and settle the filling. Repeat until all the moneybags have been made.

Line several tiers of a steamer with banana leaves or parchment paper. Arrange the moneybags on the leaves—do not crowd them. Steam over simmering water (the steamer should be at least 1 inch above the water) for about 7–10 minutes, refilling with boiling water as necessary. Serve hot with a simple dip of soy sauce.

*Note Packages of wonton wrappers vary, but most contain about 40 large (4-inch) or 70 small (3-inch) wrappers. Leftover wrappers can be frozen.

4 large pieces dried black fungus

1 bundle beanthread vermicelli noodles, about 1 oz. (see page 13)

4 slices bacon (optional)

1 lb. ground pork

1 onion, finely chopped

3–6 large garlic cloves, crushed with salt

1 tablespoon sugar

3 tablespoons fish sauce, preferably Vietnamese

1 tablespoon Szechuan peppercorns or black peppercorns, coarsely crushed

3 large eggs, beaten

2 small medium-hot red chiles, finely sliced (optional)

Golden Topping (optional)

2 egg yolks

1 tablespoon peanut oil

To serve (optional)

a large bunch of fresh herbs, such as mint, cilantro, and Asian basil

baby lettuce leaves

baguettes, split lengthwise

2–4 small red chiles, finely sliced

a loaf pan, terrine, or soufflé dish, brushed with peanut oil

Serves 4

The French colonial period made the Vietnamese master bakers, and their pâtés, too, show French influence, albeit with a decidedly local emphasis. Luc Votan, whose recipe this is, often serves the pâté in baguettes with salad, or on toast.

Vietnamese Pork Pâté with Fresh Herbs

Put the fungus into a heatproof bowl and cover with boiling water. Let stand for about 10 minutes, drain, squeeze dry in a cloth, and chop coarsely. (Remove the hard center stem first.) Put the noodles into a heatproof bowl and cover with hot water. Let stand for about 5 minutes, drain, and chop into 3-inch lengths.

Preheat a wok or skillet, add the bacon, if using, and stir-fry until crispy. Put the pork, onion, garlic, sugar, fish sauce, pepper, bacon, and beaten eggs into a food processor and blend until smooth. Transfer to a bowl and mix in the noodles, fungus, and chiles, if using.

Spoon the mixture into the prepared pan or dish and cover with foil. Tie kitchen twine around the top and steam over simmering water for about 25–50 minutes (depending on the depth of the dish). Top up with extra boiling water as required. Test by putting a chopstick into the middle of the pâté: if liquid shows in the hole, cook it longer.

To make the optional golden topping for the cooked pâté, put the egg yolks and oil into a bowl, beat well, then brush evenly over the surface of the pâté. Steam for a few minutes until the egg sets.

Serve in lettuce leaves, topped with herb leaves and sliced chiles, if using, or in baguettes with lettuce and herbs. Like most pâtés, this one is very good chilled and served the next day.

Note The pâté is also very easy to make when cooked in a microwave at 30–35 percent power for about 15–20 minutes. Test as above.

Rice

This is an easy banana leaf version of a more complicated traditional recipe using dried lotus leaves. You can also use a simple foil package.

Rice Packages

4 dried shiitake mushrooms

1½ cups jasmine rice

1 inch fresh ginger, sliced

2 tablespoons peanut oil

8 slices bacon, sliced crosswise

2 eggs

8 pieces banana leaf or dried lotus leaf soaked in boiling water until supple, or foil, 8 inches square

Flavor Mixture

1 tablespoon mirin, Shaohsing (rice wine), or dry sherry

1 tablespoon dark soy sauce

1 tablespoon oyster sauce

a pinch of sugar

1 teaspoon sesame oil

Makes 8

Put the mushrooms into a bowl, cover with boiling water, and let soak for 30 minutes. Drain, remove and discard the stems, and finely slice the caps.

To make the flavor mixture, put the mirin, soy and oyster sauces, sugar, and sesame oil into a bowl, mix well, then set aside.

Put the rice and ginger into a saucepan and add enough water to come one finger's joint above the top of the rice. Bring to a boil, cover, and cook for 8 minutes until the rice is partially cooked. Drain and discard the ginger.

Heat the oil in a wok, add the bacon, and stir-fry until crisp. Remove and set aside. Put the eggs into a bowl and beat with 1 tablespoon water. Reheat the bacon fat in the wok and swirl it so the sides are well coated, adding a little oil if necessary. Add the beaten eggs and swirl around to form a thin omelet. Cook until just set, then roll up the omelet, transfer to a plate, and slice finely.

Put the banana leaf, lotus leaf, or foil squares onto a work surface, put 1–2 tablespoons of rice in the center, then a share of all the other ingredients, including the flavor mixture. Fold up into square packages, tie with twine or thread or secure with toothpicks, and set in a steamer. Steam for about 20 minutes, then serve, cutting a cross in the top of each package just before serving, so the aromas escape across the table.

Variation Other ingredients may also be added to the rice—try cooked shredded duck, chicken, stir-fried pork strips, or the Chinese grilled pork on page 44.

Steamed Rice

Though not technically steaming, the first recipe (right) uses the absorption method—the traditional way of cooking rice in many Asian countries. It's foolproof, and it doesn't seem to matter how much rice you're cooking. The result is light, fluffy, and as separate as the variety of rice demands.

Sticky rice, the glutinous variety used in Lao, Thai, and Vietnamese cooking, especially for sweet dishes, should always be steamed. Glutinous rice, by the way, does NOT contain gluten.

If you have access to a Southeast Asian store, you may be able to buy the conical woven bamboo rice steamers used in Cambodia. The bamboo, which should be properly soaked before use, is said to give a special flavor to the sticky rice, much appreciated by aficionados.

Southeast Asian black rice can be boiled in a saucepan in the usual way (it takes much longer than white rice), but steaming is a traditional method that keeps all the flavors—none disappears into the cooking water. Sometimes, white and black rice are steamed together, and the purple-black color seeps into the white, giving a beautiful effect.

Steamed Rice

1 cup fragrant Thai rice, or jasmine rice, washed and drained

Put the rice into a saucepan and add water to one finger's joint above the level of the rice. Bring to a boil, cover with a lid, reduce the heat to the lowest possible, and let steam until done, about 12 minutes. Let rest, covered, for another 10 minutes. The rice will be perfectly dry.

Steamed Sticky Rice

1 cup sticky rice, also known as glutinous rice

Put the rice into a bowl and rinse, changing the water several times, until the water runs clear. Cover the rice with cold water, put into the refrigerator, and let soak overnight.

When ready to cook, drain the rice, then line a steamer with cheesecloth or prepare a soaked bamboo steamer (see recipe introduction, left). Cover and steam for about 45 minutes until done. Remove from the heat and fluff up with a fork.

Steamed Black Rice

1 cup Asian black rice

Put the rice into a bowl, cover with cold water, and let soak for at least 4 hours, or overnight in the refrigerator.

When ready to cook, drain the rice, then line a steamer with cheesecloth, or prepare a soaked bamboo rice steamer (see recipe introduction, left). Steam the rice for about 1 hour, or until tender. Remove from the heat and fluff up with a fork.

Black rice may also be cooked by the absorption method (above), for 25–30 minutes, using at least 2 cups water.

Note One cup uncooked rice produces about 4 cups cooked.

Sweet Things

Black rice in coconut milk is a traditional Southeast Asian sweet dish. I think it is even more delicious teamed with red fruits. Cherries and raspberries aren't tropical fruits however, so feel free to use alternatives such as papaya or lychees.

Black Rice
with Red Fruits

1 cup Asian black rice

red fruits, such as cherries, halved and pitted, or raspberries (red or golden), to serve

Coconut Ginger Syrup

2 cups coconut cream*

¼ cup brown sugar

1 inch fresh ginger, peeled and grated

a pinch of salt

Serves 4

Put the rice into a bowl, cover with cold water, and let soak for at least 4 hours, or overnight in the refrigerator.

When ready to cook, drain the rice, then line a steamer with cheesecloth, or prepare a soaked bamboo rice steamer (see recipe introduction, page 54). Steam the rice for about 1 hour, or until tender. Remove from the heat and fluff up with a fork.

To make the sauce, put the coconut cream into a small saucepan, add the sugar and grated ginger, and bring to a boil until the sugar has dissolved.

Add the cooked rice to the pan and simmer until thick. Let cool but do not chill. When cool, serve topped with the fruit.

*Note Coconut cream is the thick part of coconut milk. It is sold separately, or can be spooned off the top of a can of regular coconut milk. It is NOT cream of coconut, which is sold in a solid block, and is, in my opinion, very oily.

Tropical Chile Fruits in Paper Packages

2 ripe mangoes

1 ripe papaya

1 ripe banana

1 teaspoon crushed dried chiles, or to taste

sour cream, whipped cream, or crème fraîche, to serve

Sugar Lime Sauce

¼ cup brown sugar or palm sugar

grated zest and juice of 3 limes

¼ cup thick coconut cream (see note page 57)

4 sheets wax paper or foil, about 12 inches square

Serves 4

When I first saw fresh fruit sprinkled with chile powder sold in street markets in India, I thought it was a crazy idea (not being a chile fan at that time). Then, bravely, one day I tried it. It was terrific. This recipe is a delicious, easy way to end a meal: heating intensifies the fruit taste and the chile gives a delicious spark (perfect with sweet things). Remember, you're not cooking the fruit, just warming it to develop the flavors.

Peel and pit the mangoes. Peel and seed the papaya. Cut both fruit into short slices or ¾-inch cubes. Slice the banana.

To make the sugar lime sauce, put the sugar, lime juice, and coconut cream into a small saucepan and simmer until the sugar has dissolved. Take the 4 squares of wax paper or foil. Put the fruit in piles in the center of each square. Sprinkle the sugar lime sauce on top, then sprinkle with the chiles and lime zest. Close and seal the packages and steam for about 5 minutes, or just until heated through. You aren't cooking the fruit, merely heating it.

Serve in the packages with a separate bowl of cream.

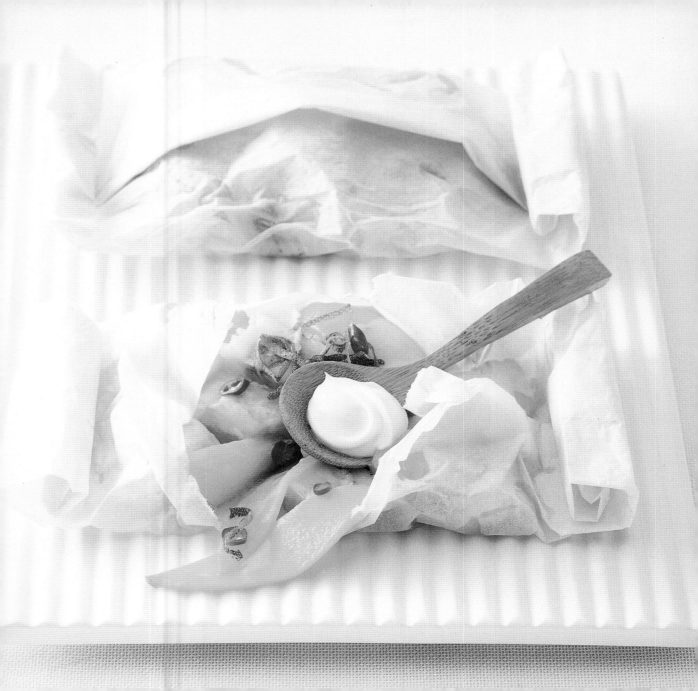

Pumpkin is a chameleon—it can be sweet or savory, and here it's sweet. In Southeast Asia, this custard is usually made with duck eggs (a gang of ducks with a small boy herding them off into the fields for the day is a common sight). If pumpkins are scarce, you can cook these simple puddings in ordinary timbale molds.

Pumpkin Puddings

1 small pumpkin, such as kabochka or buttercup, or 4 baby pumpkins, all with little stalks if possible.

Coconut Custard

4 hen eggs or 3 duck eggs

1 cup brown sugar or palm sugar, if available, plus extra, to serve

1 cup coconut cream (see note page 57)

Serves 4

Cut out the top of the pumpkin(s) and, using a melon baller or small ice cream scoop, remove and discard the seeds and membranes. Put the pumpkin(s) onto a plate that will fit inside a bamboo steamer.

To make the coconut custard, put the eggs into a heatproof bowl and beat well. Add the sugar and stir until smooth and thick, then stir in the coconut cream. Put the bowl over a saucepan of simmering water and heat gently (you're not cooking it, just warming it to make it ready for steaming).

Put the pumpkin(s), in their steamers, on top of a pan of boiling water. Pour the coconut custard into the pumpkins. If you have any left over, put into small bowls or timbale molds. Put a covering of cheesecloth over the custards so they don't fill with water dripping off the top of the steamer lid. If you have kept the pumpkin tops, add to the steamer (they will cook more quickly than the puddings, so remove when done).

Cook over a steady steam for about 45 minutes to 1 hour until the custard has puffed a little and is firm on the surface, but still wobbly in the middle. Put a knife or chopstick into the middle of the custard: it should come out clean.

Serve on small plates, with an extra sprinkle of sugar, if using. Serve cool or cold. If you've used a large pumpkin, serve it cut into wedges like a cake.

Variation Some recipes use a few drops of kewra water to flavor the pudding. Kewra water, found in Indian stores, is made from pandanus or screwpine, and has a delicious flowery scent. The Thai version, called *toey*, is very strong, so you should use just a little. These ingredients are not crucial, but worth trying if you see them in a speciality store.

In Cambodia, sticky rice is cooked in a woven bamboo basket steamer set over a pot a little like a *couscousière*. There is a Vietnamese old wives' tale that if you don't look after your stomach, when you get old, you'll have to eat sticky rice— so presumably it's easy to digest.

Sticky Rice with Mango

1 cup sticky rice, also known as glutinous rice

1 cup coconut milk

¼ cup white sugar

a small pinch of salt

2 ripe mangoes

Serves 4

Put the rice into a bowl and rinse, changing the water several times, until the water runs clear. Cover the rice with cold water, put into the refrigerator, and let soak overnight.

When ready to cook, drain the rice, then line a steamer with cheesecloth or prepare a soaked bamboo steamer (see recipe introduction, page 54). Cover and steam for about 45 minutes until done. Remove from the heat and fluff up with a fork.

Meanwhile, to prepare the mangoes, cut the cheeks off either side of the pit and cut a checkerboard in the flesh without going through the skin. Lift off the diced mango with a fork. Peel the remaining skin off the mango, then dice the remaining flesh (or eat as the cook's treat).

Transfer the cooked rice to a saucepan, add the coconut milk, sugar, and salt, and cook until the sugar has dissolved and the rice is thick. Serve in bowls, topped with the mango.

Note It is traditional to chill the mango, but I think that fruit has more flavor at room temperature. Also, never put fruit into the refrigerator for more than 30 minutes or so—if they're tropicals, you'll give them frostbite!

Variation **Sticky Rice Cake with Palm Sugar Syrup** Spoon the cooked sticky rice into a nonstick springform cake pan and let set. Don't refrigerate (it can be left in the pan for several hours). To make the syrup, dissolve about ¼ cup palm sugar or brown sugar in ¼ cup hot water. To serve, remove the cake from the pan, cut into wedges, and put onto serving plates. Drizzle the sugar syrup over the top and serve with mango.